OUR COURT SYSTEM

Zachary A. Kelly

The Rourke Corporation, Inc.
Vero Beach, Florida 32964

PHOTO CREDITS:
Danny Bachelor: cover, pages 4, 30, 33, 44; © Franz Jantzen/Collection of the Supreme Court of the United States: page 6; East Coast Studios: pages 7, 14, 20, 32; © Bob Daemmrich/Stock Boston: pages 9, 28; © Reuters/Brian Snyder/Archive Photos: page 12; Tony Gray: page 16; © Stephen Frisch/Stock Boston: page 22; © Stock Boston: page 24; © Rhoda Sidney/Stock Boston: page 35; © Peter Menzel/Stock Boston: page 38; © Jim Pickerell/Stock Boston: pages 40, 42

PRODUCED BY: East Coast Studios, Merritt Island, Florida

EDITORIAL SERVICES:
Penworthy Learning Systems

Library of Congress Cataloging-in-Publication Data

Kelly, Zachary A., 1970-
    Our court system / by Zachary Kelly.
       p. cm. — (Law and order)
    Includes index.
    Summary: Explains elements of the justice system including the kinds of courts; the roles of attorneys, judges, and jurors; pretrial arraignments; preliminary hearings; and trials.
    ISBN 0-86593-575-0
    1. Courts—United States Juvenile literature. 2. Procedure (Law)—United States Juvenile literature. [1. Courts. 2. Law.] I. Title. II. Series.
KF8720.K43   1999
347.73'1—dc21   99-28687
                                                  CIP

Printed in the USA

TABLE OF CONTENTS

Courthouses may be found in all types of buildings—some modern, some historic.

CHAPTER ONE

TWO KINDS OF COURT

What is a court? A court is a place where government carries out laws and settles disagreements between people. There are two kinds of courts. The **criminal court** works with people accused of a crime. After police investigate a crime, they bring the suspect to court. There the suspect can go to trial to prove his or her innocence or guilt. The **civil court** is for people or groups who disagree about their rights. A judge or jury helps settle the disagreement between two people who disagree. Criminal and civil courts are alike in many ways.

Columns and bronze doors of the U.S. Supreme Court building

People in civil and criminal courts have similar jobs. In both courts, a judge leads trials and often gives a judgment at the end. In both courts, attorneys tell their sides of the case. Both courts hold trials in much the same way. For example, in both courts the person who accuses another has to prove something and is called the **plaintiff**. The **defendant** is seen as innocent until proven guilty. Both courts use juries to help decide cases.

The prosecuting and defense attorneys view a witness' documents.

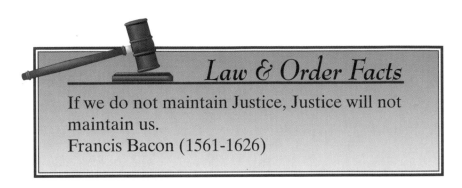

A jury is a group of local people called together to listen to the facts of a case and decide whether the defendant is guilty. Juries are made up of adult U.S. citizens, like your parents or teachers. Someday you may even be called to serve on a jury. The courtrooms of criminal and civil courts look alike. Every courtroom has a place of honor for the judge. A courtroom also has a separate place for each side's attorney to tell about the case. It has a witness stand for witnesses, too. Courtrooms also have a place where the jury sits and listens, and an area where visitors may sit to watch trials.

Jurors need to pay close attention at all times during a trial. The decision of guilty or not guilty is theirs.

The courts differ in who starts the case, or **prosecutes**. In criminal cases, the state prosecutes the accused person. In civil cases, the plaintiff prosecutes the other person or group. Civil cases and criminal cases both end with a **verdict**. A verdict is the finding of a jury or judge. But the verdicts are different for civil and criminal cases. In a criminal case, the verdict can put the criminal in jail for a few months or for life. In a civil case, the verdict is often an amount the defendant must pay. A civil verdict never involves jail time.

CHAPTER TWO

CRIMINAL COURT

The criminal court is one of the most powerful tools we have to enforce laws. Through it the government punishes wrongdoers and protects us, often by sending criminals to prison. The court punishes criminals only after police have investigated the case. The court must make certain that the accused person committed the crime before he or she is punished. The court also must lay down a punishment that fits the crime. Being certain is the key.

Police gather evidence to be used by the prosecution in a court of law.

A suspect is presumed (thought to be) innocent until proven guilty. Even after police are sure a certain person committed a crime, the court treats the suspect as innocent until it reads the verdict. The court places the burden of proof on the prosecution, or plaintiff. It is up to the prosecution (attorneys working for the plaintiff) to make a case and prove that the defendant is guilty beyond a reasonable doubt. All the defense (attorneys working for the defendant) has to do is point out weaknesses in the prosecution's case until the judge or jury doubts that the accused is guilty.

In court, the prosecution always gives evidence and calls witnesses first. Then the defense only has to make a witness look foolish or confused to raise doubt.

Attorneys give information about a case for the jury and judge to decide whether the defendant is guilty. The prosecution tries hard to prove the defendant guilty. The defense attorney works as hard as he or she can to protect the defendant's rights by raising doubt.

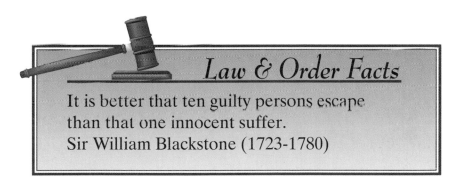

Law & Order Facts

It is better that ten guilty persons escape than that one innocent suffer.
Sir William Blackstone (1723-1780)

Attorneys on both sides make statements to the court. They both call witnesses and question each other's witnesses. Also, both attorneys give physical evidence to support their statements. Afterwards, they leave the verdict in the hands of the judge or jury.

An attorney makes his opening statement to the court.

CHAPTER THREE

ARRAIGNMENT

Several million people are arrested each year. Fewer than 100,000 go to trial. Many cases are settled at the **arraignment** before the trial. The arraignment is a meeting between the accused, the prosecuting attorney, and a judge. The accused also may have a lawyer at the arraignment. This meeting begins the criminal court process. After a suspect is arrested and written up by the police, he or she may be held in a jail until the arraignment.

A police officer must file a report and inform the accused that he or she is charged with a crime.

During this time, the police officer handling the case charges the suspect. A charge names the wrongdoing that led to the arrest. The prosecutor may go over the charge and add to it. Usually within 48 hours of arrest, a defendant stands before a judge.

An arraignment is like a little court hearing. The defendant hears the charge against him or her. After the judge reads the charge, the defendant must give a plea. A plea is the defendant's answer to the charge. There are four pleas that suspects can give. One plea is "not guilty." A suspect who pleads "not guilty" means, "No, I did not commit the crime named in the charge." Another plea is "not guilty by reason of insanity." The suspect making this plea means,"I was not in my right mind (sane) when the crime was committed." A suspect can plead "**nolo contendere**," or "no contest." It means, "I do not wish to plead 'guilty' or 'not guilty.' I will accept the court's decision." When the charge is read, a suspect can answer "Guilty." This plea means, "Yes, I did it."

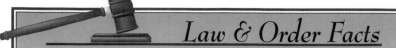

Only about half of the states allow the plea of *nolo contendere*, and even those states require the consent of the court for the plea to be accepted.

A "guilty" plea lets the judge set a sentence, and keeps the case from going to trial. Some defendants enter a *plea bargain*. A plea bargain is an agreement between the defense and prosecutor. The defendant pleads guilty if the prosecutor lowers the charge. The prosecutor drops a serious charge if the defendant pleads guilty to the lower charge.

After the plea, the judge reads the defendant's rights: the right to a defense attorney, the right to remain silent, and the right to reasonable bail. The judge may set bail now. If the suspect pays it, he or she may go home until the hearing. If the bail is not paid, the suspect stays in jail until the trial. When the accused shows up for the trial, the bail money is given back.

CHAPTER FOUR

HEARING

The hearing meets about 20 days after the arraignment. At the hearing, the judge says whether enough evidence has been found for the case to go to trial. First, the judge reviews the charge against the defendant and then reviews the bail. Next, the prosecution brings in witnesses and questions them. The defense also questions, or cross-examines, them.

The defense has a right to know the facts on which the prosecution is building its case. Sometimes the defense does not want this hearing because they think it will hurt the defendant's case. If the defense asks not to have a hearing, the judge will cancel it.

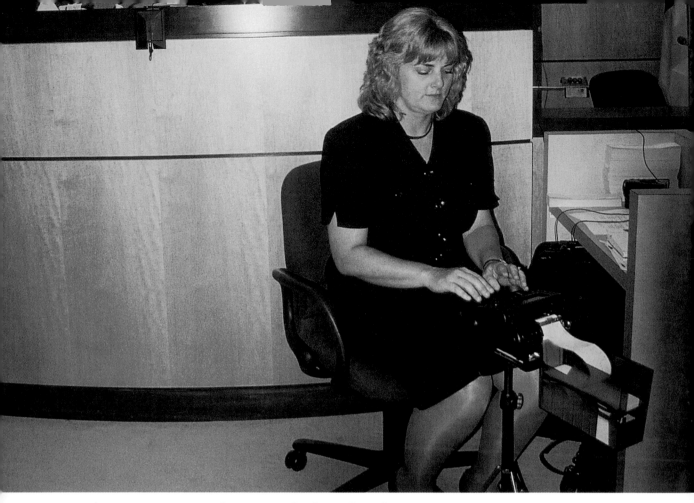

A court reporter takes notes during a hearing.

A hearing is much like a court trial. The prosecutor gives enough evidence to show the judge that the defendant might be guilty. The prosecutor saves other evidence for the trial.

Everything at the hearing is written down. The paper may be used later in the trial. If a witness forgets a fact, it can be looked up in the paper. Problems often come up in trials. The hearing write-up can help solve many of them.

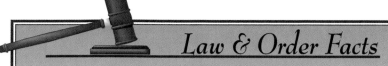

The prosecution starts a hearing by bringing witnesses to the judge. The witnesses answer questions from the prosecution. Then they answer questions from the defense if the defense chooses to cross-examine the witnesses. The defense attorneys may disagree with the prosecution's evidence. If the defense thinks the evidence should not be used in the trial, they can tell the judge. The judge decides whether the evidence can be used.

The defense also may ask the judge for a **discovery**. If the judge gives it, the prosecution must tell the evidence and statements to be used in the trial and some of the main witnesses. The defense has a right to know how the prosecution has built the case and how they will present it in court. A discovery is a way of being fair to the defendant and his or her attorneys.

A defense lawyer presents her case to the judge for a discovery .

CHAPTER FIVE

TRIAL

A suspect has a right to a speedy trial. The trial must happen soon after the suspect is arrested. (The U.S. Constitution gives this right, in the sixth amendment.) In many states, the court must try a suspect within 150 days. If a defendant wants a jury trial, he or she must ask for it in most states. Then the court picks local citizens to be on the jury. The jury is chosen *at random*. They are picked by chance, not by plan. Most juries have 12 people. To give a verdict, all 12 must vote the same. A defendant may ask for a **bench trial**.

The prosecution sometimes uses a police officer to explain evidence to the court.

In a bench trial, there is no jury. The judge gives the verdict. A bench trial often works in favor of the defendant.

The judge *swears in* the jury. The jurors promise to listen to facts during the trial. Then the judge reads the charge against the defendant. Next, the prosecuting attorney makes an opening statement. The defense attorney may make an opening statement, too. Or the defense may wait until the prosecution presents the whole case. The prosecution gives its evidence first, using witnesses and physical evidence. The prosecuting attorney does not give evidence, but asks questions of the witnesses.

The questions must be clear and relate to the case. The witnesses must be *competent*. Each witness must be able or fit to give evidence. If not, the defense may *object* to the evidence. (If the defense objects, the judge must say whether the evidence can be used.) After a prosecutor questions a witness, the defense may cross-examine the witness.

Then the defense may present their case. (The defense attorney may think the prosecution's evidence did not make the jury believe the defendant is guilty. If so, the defense may choose not to present a case.) The defense attorney may make an opening statement before calling a witness and giving physical evidence.

Many defense cases are built on an *alibi*: The defendant was some place else when the crime was committed. Some cases are built on *self-defense*: The defendant did what was necessary to protect himself or herself from serious harm. Defense cases may be built on *insanity*: The defendant was not sane (in his or her right mind) when the crime was committed. After the defense presents its case, the prosecution may rebut (point out flaws in the defense's case). The defense may respond one time to the prosecution. Then each side gives *closing statements*. After that, the jury gives a verdict.

CHAPTER SIX

CIVIL COURT

The purpose of the civil court is to determine the rights of two people or groups who disagree in some important way. The civil court is a way for people to settle disagreements with one another. The court and its workers do not investigate, do not question, and do not hunt for clues. The plaintiff and defendant bring their own evidence. The civil court decides the case as it is given by the plaintiff's and defendant's attorneys.

An attorney presents evidence to a jury.

Suppose a man or woman buys a car, not knowing that it's broken and cannot be fixed. And the dealer will not take it back or pay for the repairs. The buyer might take action to get the money for a new car. The action is a **lawsuit**. The money, called **retribution**, is for a wrong (selling a car that cannot be fixed). This lawsuit leads to a jury trial. The buyer and the car dealer give evidence to the court. Evidence may be in the form of papers, spoken words, and physical evidence.

A civil lawsuit may lead to a bench trial (judge alone hears the case). A couple asking the court for a divorce often will have a bench trial, not a jury trial. Also, a store asking the court for money from a nonpaying customer will have a bench trial.

The verdict in a civil case is like a criminal court verdict. The verdict is legally binding in both courts. In both courts, the verdict finds one side *at fault* and gives a sentence to match the wrong. The verdicts in either court may be appealed to a higher court. The two courts are also different. While a jury in a civil trial gives the verdict, the judge has the final say. The jury can give a verdict only within the limits set by the judge. The judge can overrule the jury (give his or her own verdict in the case).

This police officer investigates a civil crime.

CHAPTER SEVEN

PLAINTIFF AND DEFENDANT

A plaintiff starts a lawsuit for one reason: to prove that the defendant wronged the plaintiff and owes something for it. The plaintiff does not care whether the wrong was a crime. He or she just wants retribution (money) from the defendant for the wrong. The defendant may try to prove that no wrong was done and no money is due.

Often, though, civil cases can be settled outside of court. This happens when a plaintiff and defendant agree on a way to settle. For example, they may agree that the defendant will pay part of the money the plaintiff asked for. If they cannot agree, then the case must go to trial.

All courtrooms are protected by a law enforcement officer known as a bailiff.

Before starting a lawsuit, a plaintiff must find a court that has jurisdiction. The court must be in the same place as the property in the case. (Often the defendant, too, must be in the same jurisdiction.) The court also must be the kind that settles cases like the plaintiff's case. Say the plaintiff lent a new car to the defendant and he or she wrecked it. A small-claims court (takes cases where retribution is a few thousand dollars or less) would not be the right kind.

A judge listens to the plaintiffs make their case.

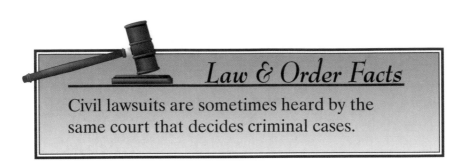

Next the plaintiff must make a *complaint*, which his or her attorney puts in writing. The complaint tells how much money the plaintiff wants or names another kind of retribution.

The plaintiff's attorney sends a paper, called a **summons**, to the defendant. A summons tells the defendant to be in court on a certain day and time. The defendant has several choices. He or she may choose not to show up in court. If so, the judge likely will say the plaintiff gets the retribution he or she asked for. The defendant may go to court, admit the wrong, and pay what the plaintiff asks. The defendant may talk to the plaintiff before the court date and settle the case.

Serving a summons is a law enforcement officer's duty.

If the defendant thinks the plaintiff does not have a good case, he or she may ask to have the case dismissed, or stopped. The defendant may write an answer to the plaintiff's complaint. The answer tells why the plaintiff should not get retribution. And it tells why the plaintiff should pay the defendant, instead of the other way around.

CHAPTER EIGHT

PLEADING

In a civil case, both the plaintiff and the defendant send papers, called **pleadings**, to the court. A pleading gives facts and asks for action. It also tells the point of view of the person who sent it. Pleadings are sent from the court to other people in the case. These papers go back and forth before a trial and may be used to work out an agreement. Many people settle their cases this way. A lawsuit that is not settled in pleading almost always goes to trial.

If you believe you have been wronged, an attorney likely will be able to help you.

The plaintiff's first pleading is called a complaint. A complaint tells a defendant what the plaintiff thinks the defendant has done wrong. It names the law that the plaintiff thinks the defendant broke. A complaint is taken to the defendant, along with a summons. A summons tells the defendant to go to court about the case on a certain day and time.

Then the plaintiff sends another pleading, called a **petition**. A petition asks the court to begin a hearing.

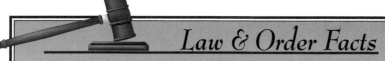

A defendant may send a pleading, too. One pleading is a **demurrer**. A demurrer says that the plaintiff's facts may be true, but the law in the case does not say the plaintiff should win with those facts. Another pleading is the answer. An answer says that some of the plaintiff's facts are not true, but the law is the right one for the case. Still another pleading is a reply. A reply says that the plaintiff's facts are true and the law is right for the case, but other facts show that the defendant does not owe the plaintiff.

Often a defendant and plaintiff trade pleadings until they settle the case outside of court. If not, they go to trial.

These lawyers work out a settlement to avoid going to court.

CHAPTER NINE

SETTLEMENT OR TRIAL

There are many ways to settle a case before it goes to court. Most people in lawsuits end up settling out of court. It takes a lot of questions and answers from both sides—a lot of give and take for an out-of-court settlement to be fair. People often agree during the pleading step. Many settle just after the defendant gets the summons. People may choose to go to trial to talk about facts of the case and rights of the plaintiff and defendant.

A jury's foreperson reads the verdict to the court.

In a civil trial the first step is to pick the jury and swear them in. Then the plaintiff begins the opening statements. The plaintiff tells the jury his or her side of the case. The defendant then tells the other side. After the opening statements, the plaintiff gives evidence about the case. This evidence will hold up the plaintiff's side of the case—what he or she told the jury. The plaintiff may call witnesses and use physical evidence. The defendant may think the plaintiff did not give enough evidence to finish the trial. And the defendant may ask to stop the trial.

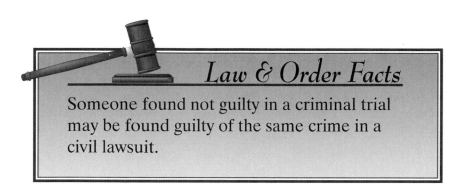

If the judge agrees, then the trial is over. If not, then the defendant gives evidence to hold up his or her side of the case.

After the defendant gives evidence, the trial cannot be stopped. If one side clearly did not prove its case, and the evidence points to the other side, the plaintiff or defendant may ask the judge for a verdict. The judge may agree that one side did not prove its case, or the judge may ask to hear closing statements from both sides. After closing statements, the case goes to the jury. Even if the jury returns with a verdict, the judge might overturn it and give a different verdict.

The judge will tap the gavel to declare a case closed, or decided.

GLOSSARY

arraignment (uh RAYN munt) — meeting of accused person and a criminal court judge in which the accused answers the charge against him or her

bench trial (BENCH TRIE ul) — case decided by a judge rather than by a jury

civil court (SIV ul KAWRT) — court that hears cases about the rights of people who disagree; not a criminal court

criminal court (KRIM uh nul KAWRT) — court that hears a case when a crime has been committed

cross-examine: (KRAWS ig ZAM in) — question a witness after the side that called the witness does so

defendant (di FEN dunt) — accused in a criminal or civil case

demurrer (duh MER er) — pleading from the defendant in response to a complaint and summons; says plaintiff's facts are true, but that the law does not hold up the plaintiff's side of the case

discovery (duh SKUV uh ree) — information about the prosecution's case given to the defense before a trial begins

lawsuit (LAW SYOOT) — action or a case taken to a civil court to right a wrong and get retribution

GLOSSARY

nolo contendere (NO lo kun TEN duh ree) — plea of "no contest" made by a defendant in a criminal case; admits neither guilt nor innocence

petition (puh TISH un) — pleading sent by a plaintiff to a civil court, asking for a hearing

plaintiff (PLAYN tif) — person or group that starts a court case by sending a complaint (civil court) or arresting (criminal court)

pleading (PLEED ing) — paper that gives reasons for the plaintiff's or defendant's side of a case

prosecutes (PRAHS i KYOOTS) — starts a lawsuit in civil or criminal court

retribution (RET ruh BYOO shun) — money, service, punishment from a defendant to make up for wrong done to the plaintiff

summons (SUM unz) — paper telling defendant to be in court on a certain date and time for a hearing or trial

verdict (VER dikt) — finding of a jury in a trial; also judges decision; a judgment

FURTHER READING

Find out more with these helpful books and information sites:

- Brown, Lawrence. *The Supreme Court.* Washington, DC: Congressional Quarterly, 1981.
- Conklin, John E. *Criminology.* Allyn and Bacon: Needham Heights, MA, 1995.
- De Sola, Ralph. *Crime Dictionary.* New York: Facts on File, 1988.
- Hill, Gerald and Hill, Kathleen. *Real Life Dictionary of the Law.* Los Angeles: General Publishing Group, 1995.
- Janosik, Robert, ed. *Encyclopedia of the American Judicial System.* New York: Charles Scribner and Sons, 1987.
- Johnson, Loch K. *America's Secret Power (CIA).* Oxford: OUP, 1989.
- Kadish, Sanford H., ed. *Encyclopedia of Crime and Justice.* New York: The Free Press, 1983.
- McShane, M. and Williams, F., eds. *Encyclopedia of American Prisons.* New York: Garland, 1996.
- Morris, N. and Rothman, D., eds. *The Oxford History of the Prison.* Oxford: OUP, 1995.
- Regoli, Robert and Hewitt, John. *Criminal Justice.* Prentice-Hall: Englewood Cliffs, NJ, 1996.
- Renstrum, Peter G. *The American Law Dictionary.* Santa Barbara, CA: ABC-CLIO, 1991.
- Territo, Leonard and others. *Crime & Justice in America.* West: St Paul, MN, 1995.
- *The Constitution of the United States.* Available in many editions.
- *The Declaration of Independence.* Available in many editions.
- Voigt, Linda and others. *Criminology and Justice.* McGraw-Hill: New York, 1994.

- http://entp.hud.gov/comcrime.html
  Crime Prevention
  Department of Justice
  PAVNET (Partnership Against Violence Network)
  Justice Information Center
  Justice for Kids & Youth
- http://www.dare-america.com/
  Official Website of D.A.R.E.
- http://www.fightcrime.com/lcrime.htm
  Safety and Security Connection
  The Ultimate Guide to Safety and Security
  Resources on the Internet
- http://www.psrc.com/lkfederal.html
  Links to most Federal Agencies

INDEX